# LINDSEY GOES TO THE DOCTOR

Written by

DR. ABRAHAM THOMAS

Character design by

NEVA THOMAS

LIGHT AUSTRALIA

I woke up in the morning and my tummy was sore.

It was not getting better and
I felt sick too

I spoke to mum and she was ringing the Doctor’s Surgery to get an appointment.

I got scared…
Really really scared

Is the doctor going to jab me with a needle ???

I started to cry….

‘I am really scared Mum,
I don’t want to go to the Doctors’,

She said I can take cuddly bear with me to the Doctors'

That sounded like a good plan.
I was relieved to hear that
cuddly bear
is joining me too…

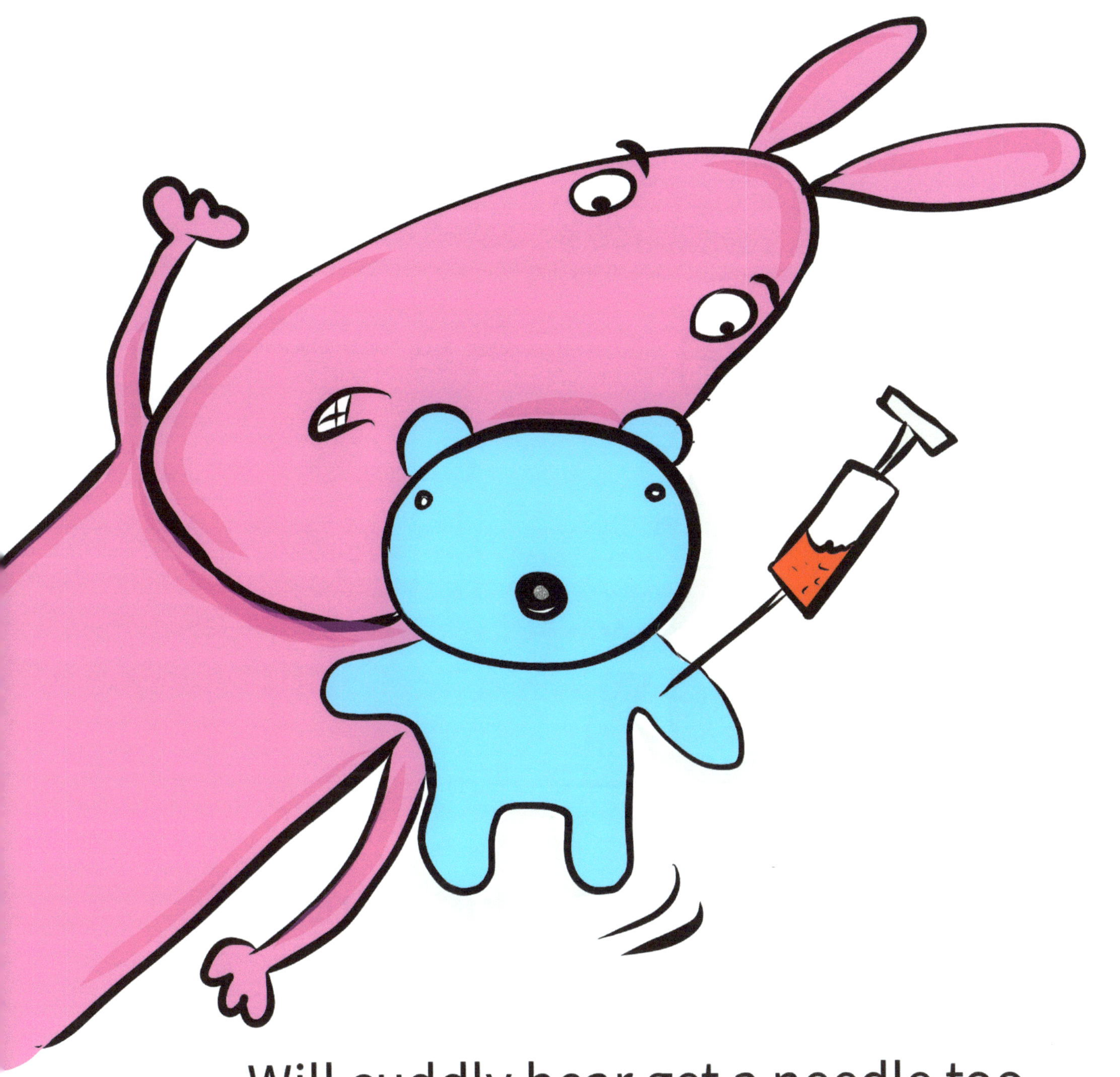

Will cuddly bear get a needle too...

Mum gave me a cuddle and
said I will be fine.
Mum assured me that
there won't be any needles.

Mum showed me a few things doctors check and we practiced on cuddly bear.

When doctor called us in,
cuddly bear went in first.

Doc Koala checked him out first…

Doc had a feel of cuddly bear’s tummy too

Then he checked me out and had a feel of my tummy . Mum and cuddly bear were next to me.

Doc gave me a bravery sticker.

Cuddly bear got one too

I was starting to feel better already!

Cuddly bear
is feeling
better too..

Doc Koala is not as scary as I thought

We waved bye to Doc Koala and ran straight to the park.

To my wonderful Neva & Aiden

First published by LIGHT AUSTRALIA  in 2022.



Design and Layout by Dr. Abraham Thomas.
Character Design by Neva Thomas



The digital  illustrations of this book is created  by Dr. Abraham Thomas & Neva Thomas.

Type set in Myriad Pro

Printed in Australia.

A catalogue record of this book is available from the National Library of Australia

www.ingramcontent.com/pod-product-compliance
Ingram Content Group UK Ltd.
Pitfield, Milton Keynes, MK11 3LW, UK
UKHW060115300726
14090UKWH00002B/208